I0436584

HOW TO START

A

NON-PROFIT

ORGANIZATION

A STEP-BY-STEP GUIDE TO NON-PROFIT STARTUP SUCCESS

Larry A. Furman

Table of contents

Introduction 6

Understanding Nonprofits 8

Key Characteristics of Nonprofits 8

Differentiating Nonprofits from For-Profits............... 9

Identifying Your Mission and Vision...................... 11

Crafting a Compelling Mission Statement 11

Defining a Clear Vision for Your Nonprofit 12

Legal Requirements and Compliance..................... 13

Steps to Register and Obtain Tax-Exempt Status...... 14

Compliance with Local and Federal Regulations...... 15

Building a Strong Board of Directors 17

Recruitment and Roles of Board Members 18

Effective Board Governance Practices 19

Strategic Planning for Success 20

Creating a Strategic Plan for Your Nonprofit........... 20

Adapting to Changing Circumstances 21

Strategic Triumphs Await...................................... 22

Fundraising Strategies 23

Developing a Comprehensive Fundraising Plan 23

Engaging with Donors and Supporters.....................................24

Ensuring Financial Sustainability..25

Budgeting and Financial Management..26

Creating a Realistic Budget 26

Financial Transparency and Accountability.............................27

Grant Management and Reporting 28

Fostering Financial Health for Long-Term Impact 28

Marketing and Outreach 30

Building a Strong Nonprofit Brand 30

Digital Marketing Strategies for Nonprofits............................31

Community Engagement and Outreach Strategies....................32

Measuring and Adapting Outreach Efforts...............................33

Building and Managing Programs..34

Designing Effective Programs Aligned with Your Mission......34

Recruiting and Managing Volunteers.......................................35

Evaluating Program Success and Impact 36

Scaling Operations and Expanding Impact 36

Sustainability and Growth..38

Financial Sustainability Strategies 38

4

Capacity Building for Organizational Resilience......................39

Adaptable Strategic Planning 40

Strategic Growth Considerations..40

Conclusion 42

The Power of Nonprofit Leadership..42

Every Challenge Is an Opportunity 42

The Heartbeat of Collaboration 43

Sustaining the Flame of Purpose 43

A Legacy of Impact 43

Introduction

In a world where purpose-driven initiatives shape communities and address societal challenges, the decision to establish a nonprofit organization is commendable and impactful.

Nonprofits are a powerful force for positive change, addressing societal gaps, and championing noble causes. From supporting vulnerable populations to advancing environmental sustainability, nonprofits are a community, a megaphone for the voiceless, a catalyst for a brighter tomorrow.

This is the magic of a nonprofit organization. It's more than just a cause; it's you, armed with unwavering conviction and a relentless drive to make a difference.

But the path to building this change-engine isn't always paved in sunshine. Doubt creeps in. Questions loom: Where do I start? How do I navigate legalities, fundraising, and team-building? How do I ensure my impact leaves a lasting ripple, not a fleeting splash?

This book is your answer. It's your launchpad, your secret weapon, your roadmap to nonprofit success. Within these pages, you'll find the battle-tested blueprint I wish I had when I first embarked on my own nonprofit journey.

In the pages ahead, we'll delve into the crucial aspects of establishing and running a nonprofit organization. From defining your mission and navigating legal requirements to building a robust board, creating impactful programs, and securing sustainable funding, each chapter provides practical, actionable insights.

Ready to articulate the essence of your nonprofit? Let your mission and vision be the rallying cry that propels your organization toward meaningful change. The pages ahead hold the keys to turning your aspirations into a reality that echoes with purpose. Your journey of impact has just begun.

Understanding Nonprofits

At the heart of every nonprofit is a mission that transcends profit margins. Unlike for-profit entities driven by financial gains, nonprofits exist to serve a purpose, often rooted in social, environmental, or community betterment. These organizations channel their resources, energy, and passion toward a cause, making a tangible impact on the world.

Key Characteristics of Nonprofits

Understanding nonprofits requires recognizing their distinctive features:

1. Mission-Driven: Nonprofits are defined by a clear and compelling mission. This mission serves as the guiding star, directing every action and decision toward the organization's overarching goal.

2. Non-Distribution Constraint: Unlike for-profit businesses that distribute profits to shareholders, nonprofits operate under a non-distribution constraint. This means that any surplus generated is reinvested back into the organization to further its mission.

3. Tax-Exempt Status: Nonprofits often enjoy tax-exempt status, meaning they are exempt from paying certain taxes. This status is contingent upon adherence to specific regulations and criteria.

4. Public Benefit: Nonprofits inherently aim to benefit the public or a particular community. Whether it's advancing education, promoting health, or addressing social issues, the focus is on creating positive change.

Differentiating Nonprofits from For-Profits

While nonprofits share some common ground with for-profit organizations, distinguishing factors include:

1. Purpose Over Profit: For-profits prioritize financial gains, while nonprofits prioritize their mission. The measure of success for a nonprofit lies in the positive impact it makes, not just the balance sheet.

2. Financial Model: Nonprofits rely on a combination of grants, donations, and other funding sources, whereas for-profits generate revenue through sales of goods or services.

3. Stakeholder Orientation: For-profits cater primarily to shareholders, seeking returns on investment. Nonprofits, on the other hand, serve the broader community and stakeholders aligned with their mission.

Identifying Your Mission and Vision

Crafting a Compelling Mission Statement

Your mission statement is the heartbeat of your nonprofit, expressing its purpose in a concise and powerful manner. Here's how you can sculpt a compelling mission statement:

1. Clarity is Key: Ensure that your mission is clear and easily understandable. Avoid jargon and intricacies; instead, aim for a statement that resonates with a broad audience.

2. Reflect Your Values: Your mission should reflect the core values that drive your organization. Consider what principles are non-negotiable and should be at the forefront of your efforts.

3. Inspire Action: A well-crafted mission inspires action. It should ignite passion, not only among your team but also among potential supporters, volunteers, and beneficiaries.

4. Be Specific, Yet Flexible: While specificity is crucial, allow room for adaptability. Your mission should guide your actions without limiting your ability to evolve and respond to changing circumstances.

Defining a Clear Vision for Your Nonprofit

If the mission is the 'why,' the vision is the 'what' — a vivid depiction of the future your nonprofit aspires to create. Here's how to define a clear vision:

1. Paint a Picture of Success: Envision the impact you aim to achieve. Describe, in tangible terms, the positive changes your nonprofit will bring about in the world.

2. Be Ambitious, Yet Realistic: Your vision should be ambitious enough to inspire, yet grounded in reality. Balance optimism with feasibility to ensure that your team and supporters believe in its attainability.

3. Align with Your Mission: Your vision and mission should be harmonious. The vision is the realization of the mission, the ultimate manifestation of the purpose your nonprofit serves.

4. Include Stakeholders: Consult with your team, board members, and key stakeholders when shaping your vision. Their insights can enrich the collective understanding of what success looks like.

Legal Requirements and Compliance

Before embarking on your nonprofit journey, it's imperative to choose a legal structure that aligns with your mission and operational goals. Common legal structures include:

1. 501(c)(3): The most prevalent choice for charitable organizations, conferring tax-exempt status. Donations to 501(c)(3) nonprofits are typically tax-deductible, enhancing fundraising potential.

2. 501(c)(4): Suited for organizations focusing on social welfare activities, advocacy, and lobbying. While donations are not tax-deductible, these nonprofits have more flexibility in political engagement.

3. 501(c)(6): Designed for business leagues, chambers of commerce, and professional associations. Contributions are not tax-deductible, but the organization can engage in some political activities.

4. Unincorporated Association and Trusts: Simplified structures suitable for smaller organizations, with fewer reporting requirements.

Understanding the nuances of each legal structure is crucial, as it forms the bedrock upon which your nonprofit's legal standing rests.

Steps to Register and Obtain Tax-Exempt Status

Navigating the bureaucratic landscape requires a systematic approach. Follow these key steps to register your nonprofit and obtain tax-exempt status:

1. Choose a Legal Name: Ensure your chosen name complies with legal requirements and is distinguishable from other organizations.

2. Draft Articles of Incorporation: Detail the fundamental aspects of your organization, including its purpose, structure, and dissolution process.

3. Appoint a Registered Agent: Designate an individual or entity responsible for receiving legal documents on behalf of your organization.

4. File for Incorporation: Submit your articles of incorporation to the appropriate state agency and pay any associated fees.

5. Apply for an EIN: Obtain an Employer Identification Number (EIN) from the IRS, a crucial identifier for your nonprofit.

6. Draft Bylaws: Clearly outline the internal rules and regulations governing your organization.

7. Apply for Tax-Exempt Status: Complete Form 1023 (or 1023-EZ for eligible organizations) to apply for federal tax-exempt status.

8. State Filings: Fulfill any additional state-specific requirements for tax-exempt status.

Compliance with Local and Federal Regulations

Compliance is an ongoing commitment essential for the smooth operation of your nonprofit. Stay vigilant by:

1. Financial Record Keeping: Maintain accurate financial records and adhere to accounting standards to ensure transparency and accountability.

2. Annual Reporting: Fulfill annual reporting requirements with both state and federal authorities, providing updates on your organization's activities and finances.

3. Governance Best Practices: Implement effective governance practices, including regular board meetings, conflict of interest policies, and adherence to ethical standards.

Building a Strong Board of Directors

A successful nonprofit board is a tapestry woven with diverse skills, experiences, and perspectives. Consider the following aspects when assembling your board:

1. Diversity Matters: Aim for diversity in gender, ethnicity, professional background, and age. A diverse board brings a richness of ideas and ensures a broader understanding of the community you serve.

2. Skill Alignment: Identify the skills your organization needs to thrive. Whether it's financial expertise, legal acumen, or marketing prowess, align board composition with the specific needs of your nonprofit.

3. Passionate Advocates: Seek individuals who are genuinely passionate about your mission. Their commitment will drive the organization forward, especially in challenging times.

4. Capacity for Collaboration: A successful board operates as a collaborative unit. Look for individuals who can contribute their expertise while working effectively with others to make collective decisions.

Recruitment and Roles of Board Members

Recruiting the right individuals is only the beginning. Once on board, each member should understand their role and responsibilities:

1. Clear Expectations: Clearly define expectations for board members, including time commitments, fundraising responsibilities, and participation in committee work.

2. Orientation and Training: Provide thorough orientation and ongoing training to help board members understand the organization's mission, operations, and their role within the broader context.

3. Committee Involvement: Distribute responsibilities through committees, allowing board members to focus on specific areas such as finance, marketing, or program oversight.

4. Term Limits and Succession Planning: Establish term limits for board members to ensure fresh perspectives and prevent stagnation. Implement a robust succession plan to facilitate smooth transitions.

Effective Board Governance Practices

Effective governance is the linchpin of a successful nonprofit. Consider these best practices:

1. Regular Board Meetings: Conduct regular and well-organized board meetings to keep members informed, engaged, and aligned with the organization's goals.

2. Transparency: Foster an environment of transparency by sharing key organizational information, including financial reports, with board members.

3. Evaluation and Feedback: Implement a system for regular board evaluations and feedback. This process helps identify strengths, areas for improvement, and opportunities for professional development.

4. Conflict of Interest Policies: Establish and adhere to conflict of interest policies to maintain the integrity of board decisions.

Strategic Planning for Success

Strategic planning is not just a management tool; it's the compass that directs your nonprofit toward enduring success.

Creating a Strategic Plan for Your Nonprofit

1. Assessing Your Current State: Begin by conducting a thorough analysis of your organization's current state. Evaluate strengths, weaknesses, opportunities, and threats (SWOT) to gain a comprehensive understanding of your internal and external landscape.

2. Defining Your Vision and Mission: Revisit and refine your mission and vision statements. Ensure they are clear, inspirational, and resonate with your stakeholders, providing a solid foundation for strategic decision-making.

3. Setting Measurable Goals and Objectives: Transform your vision into tangible goals and objectives. Each goal should be specific, measurable, achievable, relevant, and time-bound (SMART), guiding your organization toward its desired future state.

4. Engaging Stakeholders: Involve key stakeholders in the strategic planning process. Their input and perspectives can provide valuable insights, enhance buy-in, and foster a sense of collective ownership.

Adapting to Changing Circumstances

1. Flexibility and Agility: Recognize that the nonprofit landscape is dynamic. Build flexibility and agility into your strategic plan, allowing your organization to adapt to unforeseen challenges and capitalize on emerging opportunities.

2. Monitoring and Evaluation: Implement a robust monitoring and evaluation framework. Regularly assess your progress toward strategic goals, adjusting strategies as needed to stay on course.

3. Data-Informed Decision-Making: Utilize data and feedback to inform your decisions. Whether it's program impact data or feedback from stakeholders, data-driven insights enhance the effectiveness of your strategic choices.

4. Communication and Alignment: Ensure that your strategic plan is communicated clearly and consistently across your organization. Every member should understand their role in achieving the strategic goals, fostering alignment and a shared sense of purpose.

Strategic Triumphs Await

Crafting and implementing a strategic plan is not just a bureaucratic exercise; it's a dynamic process that propels your organization toward success. Chapter 5 empowers you with the tools to envision a future where your nonprofit is not just reacting to circumstances but shaping them.

As you immerse yourself in the strategic planning process, envision the impact your organization is destined to achieve. The strategic choices you make today will echo through the years, defining your nonprofit's legacy of positive change. Turn the page, and let the journey to strategic triumphs commence.

Fundraising Strategies

Assembling the financial resources necessary to bring your mission to life requires not just passion but a strategic approach that resonates with potential supporters and donors.

Developing a Comprehensive Fundraising Plan

1. Understanding Your Funding Needs: Begin by conducting a thorough assessment of your organization's financial needs. Clearly outline your budget requirements for programs, operations, and future growth.

2. Diversifying Funding Sources: Relying on a single funding source can be precarious. Explore diverse avenues such as individual donations, grants, corporate sponsorships, events, and partnerships to create a resilient financial foundation.

3. Leveraging Online Platforms and Social Media: In the digital age, online platforms and social media are powerful tools for reaching a broader audience. Establish a compelling online presence, share impactful stories, and utilize social media to connect with potential donors.

4. Crafting Persuasive Grant Proposals: For grant funding, develop clear and compelling proposals that articulate your mission, goals, and the specific impact the funding will have. Tailor proposals to align with the priorities of potential grantmakers.

Engaging with Donors and Supporters

1. Building Relationships: Fundraising is not just about transactions; it's about relationships. Cultivate meaningful connections with donors, treating them as partners in your mission rather than mere contributors.

2. Effective Donor Communication: Communicate transparently with your donors. Provide regular updates on your organization's activities, share success stories, and demonstrate the impact of their contributions.

3. Donor Recognition and Stewardship: Acknowledge and appreciate your donors. Implement a donor recognition program and stewardship initiatives to express gratitude and build a sense of belonging among your supporters.

4. Hosting Fundraising Events: Events provide not only fundraising opportunities but also a platform to engage with your community. Whether it's virtual or in-person, events can create a buzz, attract new supporters, and strengthen existing relationships.

Ensuring Financial Sustainability

1. Budgeting and Financial Transparency: Maintain a transparent and well-organized budget. Demonstrating financial responsibility builds trust with donors and ensures that funds are allocated efficiently.

2. Grant Management and Reporting: If you secure grant funding, adhere to grant reporting requirements. Provide timely and accurate reports to grantmakers, showcasing the impact of their support.

3. Planning for Long-Term Sustainability: While immediate fundraising goals are crucial, also consider the long-term sustainability of your organization. Develop a sustainable funding model that balances short-term needs with the organization's overall financial health.

Budgeting and Financial Management

An effective financial strategy not only ensures the day-to-day operations but also paves the way for sustainable growth and impactful mission execution.

Creating a Realistic Budget

1. Comprehensive Assessment: Begin by conducting a thorough assessment of your organization's financial landscape. Examine historical financial data, assess current needs, and anticipate future requirements.

2. Program and Operational Budgeting: Distinguish between programmatic and operational costs. Allocate resources strategically, ensuring that every dollar serves the overarching mission while supporting the organization's infrastructure.

3. Incorporating Contingencies: Unforeseen circumstances are inevitable. Build contingencies into your budget to address unexpected challenges or opportunities, providing financial resilience.

4. Engaging Stakeholders in the Budgeting Process: Foster transparency by involving key stakeholders, such as board members and relevant staff, in the budgeting process. Their insights and perspectives can enhance the accuracy and relevance of your financial plan.

Financial Transparency and Accountability

1. Clear Financial Reporting: Implement clear and understandable financial reporting practices. Regularly share financial statements with your board, staff, and key stakeholders, providing a transparent view of your organization's fiscal health.

2. Adhering to Accounting Standards: Maintain accurate financial records in accordance with generally accepted accounting principles (GAAP). This not only ensures compliance but also builds credibility with donors, grantmakers, and regulatory bodies.

3. Budget vs. Actual Analysis: Regularly compare budgeted figures with actual expenditures. Conducting a thorough analysis allows your organization to identify variances, learn from them, and make informed financial decisions moving forward.

4. Establishing Internal Controls: Implement internal controls to safeguard financial assets and prevent fraud. Clearly define roles and responsibilities within your financial management team to maintain accountability.

Grant Management and Reporting

1. Grant Budgeting: When managing grant funds, develop specific budgets aligned with grant requirements. Ensure that expenditures adhere to the grant's intended use and that reporting is accurate and timely.

2. Compliance with Grant Regulations: Stay informed about grant regulations and reporting deadlines. Adhering to these requirements not only ensures compliance but also positions your organization positively for future grant opportunities.

3. Impact Measurement: Demonstrate the impact of grant funds by incorporating measurable outcomes and outputs into your reporting. Showcase how the grant contributes to your organization's overall mission and goals.

Fostering Financial Health for Long-Term Impact

As you navigate the intricacies of budgeting and financial management, envision a future where your nonprofit operates with transparency, accountability, and financial resilience. This guide equips you with the tools to not only balance the books but also lay the groundwork for enduring impact. Your financial strategies today will echo through the years, shaping the narrative of your nonprofit's success. Let's embark on this journey toward fiscal health together.

Marketing and Outreach

Effectively communicating your mission and engaging with your community are paramount to achieving lasting impact and fostering sustained support.

Building a Strong Nonprofit Brand

1. Define Your Brand Identity: Clearly articulate your nonprofit's values, mission, and unique selling propositions. Your brand identity should resonate with your target audience and convey the essence of your organization.

2. Consistent Messaging: Ensure consistency in messaging across all communication channels. Whether in print, online, or in person, a unified voice enhances brand recognition and reinforces your nonprofit's core identity.

3. Visual Branding: Develop a cohesive visual identity that includes a recognizable logo, color palette, and design elements. Visual consistency enhances brand recall and contributes to a professional and cohesive image.

4. Online Presence: Establish a strong online presence through a well-designed and user-friendly website. Utilize social media platforms to share your mission, engage with supporters, and amplify your reach.

Digital Marketing Strategies for Nonprofits

1. Content Marketing: Create compelling and relevant content that tells your organization's story, showcases impact, and provides valuable information. Share this content across various platforms to build awareness and attract new supporters.

2. Email Campaigns: Develop targeted and personalized email campaigns to nurture relationships with your audience. Regular updates, newsletters, and appeals can keep supporters informed and engaged.

3. Social Media Engagement: Leverage the power of social media to connect with your community. Share impactful stories, run campaigns, and engage in conversations to build a passionate and active online community.

4. Search Engine Optimization (SEO): Optimize your website content to improve its visibility on search engines. This enhances your nonprofit's discoverability and ensures that people searching for related causes find your organization.

Community Engagement and Outreach Strategies

1. Community Partnerships: Forge partnerships with local businesses, community organizations, and other nonprofits. Collaborative efforts can amplify your impact and broaden your reach.

2. Events and Campaigns: Host events, both virtual and in-person, to bring your community together. Fundraising campaigns, awareness drives, and community gatherings provide opportunities for meaningful engagement.

3. Volunteer Engagement: Actively involve volunteers in your outreach efforts. Their passion and dedication can amplify your message, expand your network, and contribute to the success of your programs.

4. Impactful Storytelling: Share stories that resonate emotionally with your audience. Personal narratives, success stories, and testimonials create a powerful connection, making your mission more relatable and inspiring.

Measuring and Adapting Outreach Efforts

1. Data Analytics: Utilize data analytics to measure the effectiveness of your marketing and outreach efforts. Track engagement metrics, website traffic, and conversion rates to gain insights into what resonates with your audience.

2. Feedback Mechanisms: Establish feedback mechanisms to understand how your community perceives your organization. Act on feedback to refine your strategies and continuously improve your outreach initiatives.

Building and Managing Programs

Effectively designed and well-executed programs not only fulfill your organization's purpose but also create meaningful change in the communities you serve.

Designing Effective Programs Aligned with Your Mission

1. Needs Assessment: Start with a thorough needs assessment to understand the challenges and gaps in the community you aim to serve. Identify the specific needs your programs can address and tailor your interventions accordingly.

2. Goal Setting: Clearly define the goals and objectives of your programs. What specific outcomes do you aim to achieve? Goals should align with your organization's overall mission and contribute to the broader impact you envision.

3. Program Logic Model: Develop a logic model that outlines the inputs, activities, outputs, and outcomes of your programs. This visual representation helps articulate the theoretical framework behind your interventions.

4. Community Involvement: Involve the community in the program design process. Seek input from beneficiaries, community leaders, and other stakeholders to ensure that your programs are culturally sensitive and responsive to real needs.

Recruiting and Managing Volunteers

1. Volunteer Recruitment: Clearly communicate volunteer opportunities and expectations. Utilize various channels, including your website, social media, and community outreach, to attract individuals passionate about your cause.

2. Orientation and Training: Provide thorough orientation and training for volunteers. Ensure they understand your organization's mission, values, and the specific role they play in contributing to program success.

3. Recognition and Appreciation: Recognize and appreciate the contributions of volunteers. Establish a system for acknowledging their efforts, whether through volunteer appreciation events, awards, or regular expressions of gratitude.

4. Feedback Mechanisms: Create open channels for feedback from volunteers. Their insights can provide valuable perspectives on program effectiveness and areas for improvement.

Evaluating Program Success and Impact

1. Data Collection and Measurement: Implement a robust data collection system to measure program outputs and outcomes. This may include quantitative data (e.g., participant numbers) and qualitative data (e.g., success stories).

2. Continuous Monitoring: Regularly monitor program activities to ensure they align with the intended design. Identify any challenges or deviations early on and implement corrective measures as needed.

3. Participant Feedback: Solicit feedback from program participants to gauge their satisfaction and assess the perceived impact of your interventions. Act on this feedback to enhance the quality of your programs.

4. Impact Assessment: Conduct periodic impact assessments to measure the long-term effects of your programs on the community. This information is crucial for demonstrating the efficacy of your organization's efforts to stakeholders and funders.

Scaling Operations and Expanding Impact

1. Strategic Growth: Consider strategic growth opportunities based on the success and impact of your existing programs. Assess the feasibility of expanding geographically or introducing new initiatives that align with your mission.

2. Partnerships and Collaborations: Explore partnerships and collaborations with other organizations that share similar goals. Collaborative efforts can leverage collective strengths and amplify the impact of your programs.

3. Resource Mobilization: Secure the necessary resources, including funding and skilled personnel, to support program expansion. Develop a resource mobilization strategy that aligns with your growth objectives.

Sustainability and Growth

Financial Sustainability Strategies

1. Diversified Funding Streams: Strengthen financial resilience by diversifying funding sources. Relying on a mix of individual donations, grants, sponsorships, and earned revenue creates a robust financial foundation.

2. Endowment Building: Consider establishing an endowment to provide a long-term, sustainable source of income. Encourage donors to contribute to the endowment fund, ensuring ongoing financial stability.

3. Earned Income Initiatives: Explore opportunities for earned income through social enterprises, fee-for-service programs, or other revenue-generating initiatives. This diversification contributes to financial sustainability.

4. Major Gifts and Legacy Giving: Develop a major gifts program to secure substantial donations from individuals who are deeply committed to your mission. Additionally, encourage legacy giving through bequests and planned gifts to ensure future financial support.

Capacity Building for Organizational Resilience

1. Professional Development: Invest in the continuous professional development of your team. Equip staff and volunteers with the skills and knowledge needed to adapt to changing circumstances and contribute effectively to your mission.

2. Technology Integration: Leverage technology to streamline operations and enhance efficiency. Embrace digital tools for communication, fundraising, and program management, keeping your organization agile and responsive.

3. Strategic Partnerships: Cultivate strategic partnerships with other organizations, both within and outside the nonprofit sector. Collaborative efforts can maximize resources, expand your reach, and address complex challenges more effectively.

4. Board Development: Ensure a strong and engaged board of directors. Regularly assess and enhance the skills and diversity of your board, fostering a leadership team that is aligned with your organization's goals and values.

Adaptable Strategic Planning

1. Regular Strategic Reviews: Conduct regular reviews of your strategic plan. The nonprofit landscape evolves, and your organization should be nimble enough to adapt to new challenges and opportunities.

2. Environmental Scanning: Stay informed about external factors that may impact your organization. Regularly scan the environment for trends, policy changes, and emerging issues that may influence your strategic direction.

3. Feedback Loops: Establish feedback mechanisms with stakeholders, including beneficiaries, donors, and community partners. Their insights provide valuable perspectives and contribute to informed decision-making.

4. Measuring Impact: Continuously measure and communicate your organization's impact. Demonstrating the tangible outcomes of your programs enhances credibility and attracts continued support.

Strategic Growth Considerations

1. Geographic Expansion: Explore opportunities for geographic expansion if your mission aligns with addressing needs in different regions. Assess the feasibility and impact of extending your programs to new areas.

2. Programmatic Diversification: Consider diversifying your programs to address a broader range of needs within your mission scope. This strategic growth allows your organization to adapt to evolving community requirements.

3. Community Engagement: Deepen your engagement with the community you serve. Actively seek input from beneficiaries and involve them in decision-making processes, ensuring that your growth aligns with their needs and aspirations.

4. Advocacy and Policy Engagement: Engage in advocacy efforts to address systemic issues related to your mission. Advocacy can lead to policy changes that create a more supportive environment for your organization's work.

Conclusion

As we conclude, let's reflect on the profound impact your dedication and vision can have on communities and causes.

The Power of Nonprofit Leadership

Leading a nonprofit is not merely a role; it's a commitment to positive transformation. Your vision, compassion, and resilience are the driving forces that propel your organization toward meaningful change. In the pages preceding this conclusion, we've explored the fundamental elements essential to your nonprofit's success – from crafting a compelling mission to building sustainable programs and fostering growth.

Every Challenge Is an Opportunity

As you encounter challenges, remember that within each challenge lies an opportunity for innovation and growth. The nonprofit sector is dynamic, and your ability to adapt, learn, and pivot will be instrumental in overcoming obstacles and seizing opportunities. Embrace change with a spirit of curiosity, viewing every hurdle as a stepping stone toward greater impact.

The Heartbeat of Collaboration

Collaboration is the heartbeat of the nonprofit sector. Forge partnerships, both within and outside the sector, to amplify your impact. Whether through strategic alliances, community engagement, or collaborative initiatives, the collective power of shared efforts can bring about transformative change.

Sustaining the Flame of Purpose

Sustainability is not just financial; it's a commitment to purpose. As you navigate the complexities of financial management, fundraising, and strategic planning, keep the flame of your organization's purpose burning brightly. Your unwavering dedication to the mission will resonate with supporters, volunteers, and beneficiaries alike.

A Legacy of Impact

Consider the legacy you are creating. With every program, outreach effort, and strategic decision, you contribute to a legacy of positive impact. Envision a future where your nonprofit's footprint extends beyond immediate interventions, influencing the broader landscape of social change.

Dear Readers,

As you reach this conclusion, consider it not as an endpoint but as a new beginning. Your journey as a nonprofit leader is dynamic and continuous. The experiences, insights, and strategies shared here serve as stepping stones for what lies ahead.

Thank you for entrusting me as your guide on this journey. Your dedication to making a difference is the catalyst for the positive transformations our communities and the world need. As you turn the page from this conclusion, remember that every endeavor, no matter how small, contributes to the tapestry of lasting change.

May your nonprofit journey be marked by resilience, innovation, and an unwavering commitment to the betterment of our world. Here's to the impact you will create, the lives you will touch, and the legacy you will leave behind.

Wishing you continued success and fulfillment in your noble pursuit.

With sincere gratitude!

DAILY

JOURNAL

DAILY JOURNAL

_____

_____

_____

_____

_____

_____

_____

_____

_____

_____

_____

_____

_____

_____

_____

_____

DAILY JOURNAL

DAILY JOURNAL

_____

_____

_____

_____

_____

_____

_____

_____

_____

_____

_____

_____

_____

_____

_____

_____

DAILY JOURNAL

_____

_____

_____

_____

_____

_____

_____

_____

_____

_____

_____

_____

_____

_____

_____

_____

DAILY JOURNAL

DAILY JOURNAL

_____

_____

_____

_____

_____

_____

_____

_____

_____

_____

_____

_____

_____

_____

_____

_____

DAILY JOURNAL

_____

_____

_____

_____

_____

_____

_____

_____

_____

_____

_____

_____

_____

_____

_____

_____

DAILY JOURNAL

DAILY JOURNAL

DAILY JOURNAL

www.ingramcontent.com/pod-product-compliance
Lightning Source LLC
Chambersburg PA
CBHW071216290526
45796CB00008B/258